PMP® Pocket Guide

The Ultimate PMP® Exam Cheat Sheets

Based on:

A Guide to the Project Management Body of Knowledge (PMBOK® Guide) - Sixth Edition

Belinda Goodrich
PMP, PMI-RMP, PMI-SP, PgMP, PMI-ACP, CAPM

PMLearningSolutions.com
BelindaGoodrich.com

PMP® Pocket Guide – The Ultimate PMP Exam Cheat Sheets

Ordering Information:

Special discounts are available on quantity purchases by corporations, associations, educators, and others. For details, contact the publisher at the above listed web address.

Although the authors and publisher have made every effort to ensure accuracy and completeness of the information in this book, we assume no responsibility for errors, inaccuracies, omissions, or inconsistencies included herein.

Project Management Professional (PMP)®, Certified Associate in Project Management (CAPM)®, PMI Risk Management Professional (PMI-RMP)®, PMI Scheduling Professional (PMI-SP)®, Program Management Professional (PgMP)®, PMI Agile Certified Practitioner (PMI-ACP)®, A Guide to the Project Management Body of Knowledge *(PMBOK® Guide)*, Project Management Institute (PMI)®, PMI Talent Triangle®, "PMP", "CAPM", "PMI-RMP", "PMI-SP", "PgMP", "PMI-ACP", "PMBOK", "PMI", and the "PMI Registered Education Provider Logo" are registered marks of Project Management Institute, Inc. All other product names and services used throughout this course may be common law or registered trademarks of their respective proprietors.

Table of Contents

Framework / ITTOs

Key Focus Areas

Table of Contents

Process Summaries

Exam

Never stop growing, learning, and achieving. Go all in and demonstrate your experience and knowledge by pursuing goals!

Best of luck on your PMP® exam and thank you for being part of the project management community!

Belinda

This PMP® Pocket Guide is designed to give you a quick summary of all the key concepts that you will need to know to feel confident going into the Project Management Professional (PMP)® exam based on the *PMBOK® Guide, 6th Edition*, effective 26 March 2018. **It is intended to be a supplement to your PMP® exam prep course or self-study program and not a stand-alone preparation tool.**

The PMP® exam is administered by the Project Management Institute (PMI)®. Qualified, experienced project managers (PMs) can apply to PMI® to take the exam. The exam is administered at Prometric locations globally. To find a location near you visit Prometric.com/PMI.

The PMP® exam is based on the text, *A Guide to the Project Management Body of Knowledge, (PMBOK® Guide)* and "other relevant sources".

Within the *PMBOK® Guide*, PMI® presents the Project Management Framework, which you will find on the following two pages. Please note that there are:

- Ten **Knowledge Areas**
- Five **Process Groups** (groups of related processes, not phases)
- Forty-Nine **Processes**, each associated with a knowledge area and a process group

For each of the 49 processes, there are:

- **Inputs** to that process
- **Tools and Techniques** that may be used during that process
- **Outputs** from that process, many of which become inputs to other processes

These are called "ITTOs". On pages 4, 5, 6 and 7, you will see all the ITTOs for all 49 processes. They are organized by knowledge area. I do not recommend memorizing all the ITTOs; by understanding each of the 49 processes, however, the ITTOs for that process will be more intuitive. On pages 14 - 16, I provide you with a list of the common ITTOs: those that you have to understand although it is not critical to memorize which processes have them and which do not.

All the processes are described in detail starting on page 42.

As you are preparing for your exam, if you get to a page in this book that appears to be new information, cross-reference the topic with your courseware, self-study materials, or the *PMBOK® Guide* for more information.

For additional study materials, free resources, or to enroll in a convenient class, visit us at PMLearningSolutions.com.

KNOWLEDGE AREAS	PROCESS GROUPS	
	Initiating 2 processes 13% of exam	Planning 24 processes 24% of exam
Integration	• Develop Project Charter	• Develop Project Management Plan
Scope		• Plan Scope Management • Collect Requirements • Define Scope • Create WBS
Schedule		• Plan Schedule Management • Define Activities • Sequence Activities • Estimate Activity Durations • Develop Schedule
Cost		• Plan Cost Management • Estimate Costs • Determine Budget
Quality		• Plan Quality Management
Resource		• Plan Resource Management • Estimate Activity Resources
Communications		• Plan Communications Management
Risk		• Plan Risk Management • Identify Risks • Perform Qualitative Risk Analysis • Perform Quantitative Risk Analysis • Plan Risk Responses
Procurement		• Plan Procurement Management
Stakeholder	• Identify Stakeholders	• Plan Stakeholder Engagement

Project Management Institute, *A Guide to the Project Management Body of Knowledge, (PMBOK® Guide) – Sixth Edition*, Project Management Institute Inc., 2017. Page 25.

PROCESS GROUPS		
Executing 10 processes 31% of exam	**Monitoring and Controlling** 12 processes 25% of exam	**Closing** 1 process 7% of exam
• Direct and Manage Project Work • Manage Project Knowledge	• Monitor and Control Project Work • Perform Integrated Change Control	• Close Project or Phase
	• Validate Scope • Control Scope	
	• Control Schedule	
	• Control Costs	
• Manage Quality	• Control Quality	
• Acquire Resources • Develop Team • Manage Team	• Control Resources	
• Manage Communications	• Monitor Communications	
• Implement Risk Responses	• Monitor Risks	
• Conduct Procurements	• Control Procurements	
• Manage Stakeholder Engagement	• Monitor Stakeholder Engagement	

Project Management Institute, *A Guide to the Project Management Body of Knowledge, (PMBOK® Guide) – Sixth Edition*, Project Management Institute Inc., 2017. Page 25.

PROCESSES are named in a verb-noun format (ex: Develop Schedule)

PROCESS GROUPS are groups of related processes, not phases, and can occur concurrently and iteratively

	Process	Inputs	Tools & Techniques	Outputs
INTEGRATION	**Develop Project Charter**	1. Business Documents 2. Agreements 3. EEF 4. OPA	1. Expert judgment 2. Data gathering 3. Interpersonal and team skills 4. Meetings	1. Project charter 2. Assumption log
	Develop Project Management Plan	1. Project charter 2. Outputs from other processes 3. EEF 4. OPA	1. Expert judgment 2. Data gathering 3. Interpersonal and team skills 4. Meetings	1. Project management plan
	Direct and Manage Project Work	1. Project management plan 2. Project documents 3. Approved change requests 4. EEF 5. OPA	1. Expert judgment 2. Project management information system 3. Meetings	1. Deliverables 2. Work performance data 3. Issue log 4. Change requests 5. Project management plan updates 6. Project documents updates 7. OPA updates
	Manage Project Knowledge	1. Project management plan 2. Project documents 3. Deliverables 4. EEF 5. OPA	1. Expert judgment 2. Knowledge management 3. Information management 4. Interpersonal and team skills	1. Lessons learned register 2. Project management plan updates 3. OPA updates
	Monitor and Control Project Work	1. Project management plan 2. Project documents 3. Work performance information 4. Agreements 5. EEF 6. OPA	1. Expert judgment 2. Data analysis 3. Decision making 4. Meetings	1. Work performance reports 2. Change requests 3. Project management plan updates 4. Project documents updates
	Perform Integrated Change Control	1. Project management plan 2. Project documents 3. Work performance reports 4. Change requests 5. EEF 6. OPA	1. Expert judgment 2. Change control tools 3. Data analysis 4. Decision making 5. Meetings	1. Approved change requests 2. Project management plan updates 3. Project documents updates
	Close Project or Phase	1. Project charter 2. Project management plan 3. Project documents 4. Accepted deliverables 5. Business documents 6. Agreements 7. Procurement documentation 8. OPA	1. Expert judgment 2. Data analysis 3. Meetings	1. Project documents updates 2. Final product, service, or result transition 3. Final report 4. OPA updates
SCOPE	**Plan Scope Management**	1. Project charter 2. Project management plan 3. EEF 4. OPA	1. Expert judgment 2. Data analysis 3. Meetings	1. Scope management plan 2. Requirements management plan
	Collect Requirements	1. Project charter 2. Project management plan 3. Project documents 4. Business documents 5. Agreements 6. EEF 7. OPA	1. Expert judgment 2. Data gathering 3. Data analysis 4. Decision making 5. Data representation 6. Interpersonal and team skills 7. Context diagram 8. Prototypes	1. Requirements documentation 2. Requirements traceability matrix
	Define Scope	1. Project charter 2. Project management plan 3. Project documents 4. EEF 5. OPA	1. Expert judgment 2. Data analysis 3. Decision making 4. Interpersonal and team skills 5. Product analysis	1. Project scope statement 2. Project documents updates
	Create WBS	1. Project management plan 2. Project documents 3. EEF 4. OPA	1. Expert judgment 2. Decomposition	1. Scope baseline 2. Project documents updates
	Validate Scope	1. Project management plan 2. Project documents 3. Verified deliverables 4. Work performance data	1. Inspection 2. Decision-making	1. Accepted deliverables 2. Work performance information 3. Change requests 4. Project documents updates
	Control Scope	1. Project management plan 2. Project documents 3. Work performance data 4. OPA	1. Data analysis	1. Work performance information 2. Change requests 3. Project management plan updates 4. Project documents updates

Project Management Institute, *A Guide to the Project Management Body of Knowledge, (PMBOK® Guide) – Sixth Edition*, Project Management Institute Inc., 2017.

	Process	Inputs	Tools & Techniques	Outputs
SCHEDULE	**Plan Schedule Management**	1. Project charter 2. Project management plan 3. EEF 4. OPA	1. Expert judgment 2. Data analysis 3. Meetings	1. Schedule management plan
	Define Activities	1. Project management plan 2. EEF 3. OPA	1. Expert judgment 2. Decomposition 3. Rolling wave planning 4. Meetings	1. Activity list 2. Activity attributes 3. Milestone list 4. Change requests 5. Project management plan updates
	Sequence Activities	1. Project management plan 2. Project documents 3. EEF 4. OPA	1. Precedence diagramming method 2. Dependency determination and integration 3. Leads and lags 4. Project management information system	1. Project schedule network diagrams 2. Project documents updates
	Estimate Activity Durations	1. Project management plan 2. Project documents 3. EEF 4. OPA	1. Expert judgment 2. Analogous estimating 3. Parametric estimating 4. Three-point estimating 5. Bottom-up estimating 6. Data analysis 7. Decision making 8. Meetings	1. Duration estimates 2. Basis of estimates 3. Project documents updates
	Develop Schedule	1. Project management plan 2. Project documents 3. Agreements 4. EEF 5. OPA	1. Schedule network analysis 2. Critical path method 3. Resource optimization 4. Data analysis 5. Leads and lags 6. Schedule compression 7. PMIS 8. Agile release planning	1. Schedule baseline 2. Project schedule 3. Schedule data 4. Project calendars 5. Change requests 6. Project management plan updates 7. Project documents updates
	Control Schedule	1. Project management plan 2. Project documents 3. Work performance data 4. OPA	1. Data analysis 2. Critical path method 3. PMIS 4. Resource optimization 5. Leads and lags 6. Schedule compression	1. Work performance information 2. Schedule forecasts 3. Change requests 4. Project management plan updates 5. Project documents updates
COST	**Plan Cost Management**	1. Project charter 2. Project management plan 3. EEF 4. OPA	1. Expert judgment 2. Data analysis 3. Meetings	1. Cost management plan
	Estimate Costs	1. Project management plan 2. Project documents 3. EEF 4. OPA	1. Expert judgment 2. Analogous estimating 3. Parametric estimating 4. Bottom-up estimating 5. Three-point estimating 6. Data analysis 7. PMIS 8. Decision making	1. Cost estimates 2. Basis of estimates 3. Project documents updates
	Determine Budget	1. Project management plan 2. Project documents 3. Business documents 4. Agreements 5. EEF 6. OPA	1. Expert judgment 2. Cost aggregation 3. Data analysis 4. Historical information review 5. Funding limit reconciliation 6. Financing	1. Cost baseline 2. Project funding requirements 3. Project documents updates
	Control Costs	1. Project management plan 2. Project documents 3. Project funding requirements 4. Work performance data 5. OPA	1. Expert judgment 2. Data analysis 3. To-complete performance index (TCPI) 4. PMIS	1. Work performance information 2. Cost forecasts 3. Change requests 4. Project management plan updates 5. Project documents updates

Project Management Institute, *A Guide to the Project Management Body of Knowledge, (PMBOK® Guide) – Sixth Edition*, Project Management Institute Inc., 2017.

	Process	Inputs	Tools & Techniques	Outputs
QUALITY	**Plan Quality Management**	1. Project charter 2. Project management plan 3. Project documents 4. EEF 5. OPA	1. Expert judgment 2. Data gathering 3. Data analysis 4. Decision making 5. Data representation 6. Test and inspection planning 7. Meetings	1. Quality management plan 2. Quality metrics 3. Project management plan updates 4. Project documents updates
	Manage Quality	1. Project management plan 2. Project documents 3. OPA	1. Data gathering 2. Data analysis 3. Decision making 4. Data representation 5. Audits 6. Design for X 7. Problem solving 8. Quality improvement methods	1. Quality reports 2. Test and evaluation documents 3. Change requests 4. Project management plan updates 5. Project documents updates
	Control Quality	1. Project management plan 2. Project documents 3. Approved change requests 4. Deliverables 5. Work performance data 6. EEF 7. OPA	1. Data gathering 2. Data analysis 3. Inspection 4. Testing/product evaluations 5. Data representation 6. Meetings	1. Quality control measurements 2. Verified deliverables 3. Work performance information 4. Change requests 5. Project management plan updates 6. Project documents updates
RESOURCE	**Plan Resource Management**	1. Project charter 2. Project management plan 3. Project documents 4. EEF 5. OPA	1. Expert judgment 2. Data representation 3. Organizational theory 4. Meetings	1. Resource management plan 2. Team charter 3. Project documents updates
	Estimate Activity Resources	1. Project management plan 2. Project documents 3. EEF 4. OPA	1. Expert judgment 2. Bottom-up estimating 3. Analogous estimating 4. Parametric estimating 5. Data analysis 6. PMIS 7. Meetings	1. Resource requirements 2. Basis of estimates 3. Resource breakdown structure 4. Project documents updates
	Acquire Resources	1. Project management plan 2. Project documents 3. EEF 4. OPA	1. Decision making 2. Interpersonal and team skills 3. Pre-assignment 4. Virtual teams	1. Physical resource assignments 2. Project team assignments 3. Resource calendars 4. Change requests 5. Project management plan updates 6. Project documents updates 7. EEF updates 8. OPA updates
	Develop Team	1. Project management plan 2. Project documents 3. EEF 4. OPA	1. Colocation 2. Virtual teams 3. Communication technology 4. Interpersonal and team skills 5. Recognition and rewards 6. Training 7. Individual and team assessments 8. Meetings	1. Team performance assessments 2. Change requests 3. Project management plan updates 4. Project documents updates 5. EEF updates 6. OPA updates
	Manage Team	1. Project management plan 2. Project documents 3. Work performance reports 4. Team performance assessments 5. EEF 6. OPA	1. Interpersonal and team skills 2. PMIS	1. Change requests 2. Project management plan updates 3. Project documents updates 4. EEF updates
	Control Resources	1. Project management plan 2. Project documents 3. Work performance data 4. Agreements 5. OPA	1. Data analysis 2. Problem solving 3. Interpersonal and team skills 4. PMIS	1. Work performance information 2. Change requests 3. Project management plan updates 4. Project documents updates
COMMUNICATION	**Plan Communications Management**	1. Project charter 2. Project management plan 3. Project documents 4. EEF 5. OPA	1. Expert judgment 2. Communication requirements analysis 3. Communication technology 4. Communication models 5. Communication methods 6. Interpersonal and team skills 7. Data representation 8. Meetings	1. Communications management plan 2. Project management plan updates 3. Project documents updates
	Manage Communications	1. Project management plan 2. Project documents 3. Work performance reports 4. EEF 5. OPA	1. Communication technology 2. Communication methods 3. Communication skills 4. PMIS 5. Project reporting 6. Interpersonal and team skills 7. Meetings	1. Project communications 2. Project management plan updates 3. Project documents updates 4. OPA updates
	Monitor Communications	1. Project management plan 2. Project documents 3. Work performance data 4. EEF 5. OPA	1. Expert judgment 2. PMIS 3. Data representation 4. Interpersonal and team skills 5. Meetings	1. Work performance information 2. Change requests 3. Project management plan updates 4. Project documents updates

Project Management Institute, *A Guide to the Project Management Body of Knowledge, (PMBOK® Guide) – Sixth Edition,* Project Management Institute Inc., 2017.

	Process	Inputs	Tools & Techniques	Outputs
RISK	**Plan Risk Management**	1. Project charter 2. Project management plan 3. Project documents 4. EEF 5. OPA	1. Expert judgment 2. Data analysis 3. Meetings	1. Risk management plan
	Identify Risks	1. Project management plan 2. Project documents 3. Agreements 4. Procurement documentation 5. EEF 6. OPA	1. Expert judgment 2. Data gathering 3. Data analysis 4. Interpersonal and team skills 5. Prompt lists 6. Meetings	1. Risk register 2. Risk report 3. Project documents updates
	Perform Qualitative Risk Analysis	1. Project management plan 2. Project documents 3. EEF 4. OPA	1. Expert judgment 2. Data gathering 3. Data analysis 4. Interpersonal and team skills 5. Risk categorization 6. Data representation 7. Meetings	1. Project documents updates
	Perform Quantitative Risk Analysis	1. Project management plan 2. Project documents 3. EEF 4. OPA	1. Expert judgment 2. Data gathering 3. Interpersonal and team skills 4. Representations of uncertainty 5. Data analysis	1. Project documents updates
	Plan Risk Responses	1. Project management plan 2. Project documents 3. EEF 4. OPA	1. Expert judgment 2. Data gathering 3. Interpersonal and team skills 4. Strategies for threats 5. Strategies for opportunities 6. Contingent response strategies 7. Strategies for overall project risk 8. Data analysis 9. Decision making	1. Change requests 2. Project management plan updates 3. Project documents updates
	Implement Risk Responses	1. Project management plan 2. Project documents 3. OPA	1. Expert judgment 2. Interpersonal and team skills 3. PMIS	1. Change requests 2. Project documents updates
	Monitor Risks	1. Project management plan 2. Project documents 3. Work performance data 4. Work performance reports	1. Data analysis 2. Audits 3. Meetings	1. Work performance information 2. Change requests 3. Project management plan updates 4. Project documents updates 5. OPA updates
PROCUREMENT	**Plan Procurement Management**	1. Project charter 2. Business documents 3. Project management plan 4. Project documents 5. EEF 6. OPA	1. Expert judgment 2. Data gathering 3. Data analysis 4. Source selection analysis 5. Meetings	1. Procurement management plan 2. Procurement strategy 3. Bid documents 4. Procurement statement of work 5. Source selection criteria 6. Make-or-buy decisions 7. Independent cost estimates 8. Change requests 9. Project documents updates 10. OPA updates
	Conduct Procurements	1. Project management plan 2. Project documents 3. Procurement documentation 4. Seller proposals 5. EEF 6. OPA	1. Expert judgment 2. Data gathering 3. Data analysis 4. Source selection analysis 5. Meetings	1. Selected sellers 2. Agreements 3. Change requests 4. Project management plan updates 5. Project documents updates 6. OPA updates
	Control Procurements	1. Project management plan 2. Project documents 3. Agreements 4. Procurement documentation 5. Approved change requests 6. Work performance data 7. EEF 8. OPA	1. Expert judgment 2. Claims administration 3. Data analysis 4. Inspection 5. Audits	1. Closed procurements 2. Work performance information 3. Procurement documentation updates 4. Change requests 5. Project management plan updates 6. Project documents updates 7. OPA updates
STAKEHOLDER	**Identify Stakeholders**	1. Project charter 2. Business documents 3. Project management plan 4. Project documents 5. Agreements 6. EEF 7. OPA	1. Expert judgment 2. Data gathering 3. Data analysis 4. Data representation 5. Meetings	1. Stakeholder register 2. Change requests 3. Project management plan updates 4. Project documents updates
	Plan Stakeholder Engagement	1. Project charter 2. Project management plan 3. Project documents 4. Agreements 5. EEF 6. OPA	1. Expert judgment 2. Data gathering 3. Data analysis 4. Decision making 5. Data representation 6. Meetings	1. Stakeholder engagement plan
	Manage Stakeholder Engagement	1. Project management plan 2. Project documents 3. EEF 4. OPA	1. Expert judgment 2. Communication skills 3. Interpersonal and team skills 4. Ground rules 5. Meetings	1. Change requests 2. Project management plan updates 3. Project documents updates
	Monitor Stakeholder Engagement	1. Project management plan 2. Project documents 3. Work performance data 4. EEF 5. OPA	1. Data analysis 2. Decision making 3. Data representation 4. Communication skills 5. Interpersonal and team skills 6. Meetings	1. Work performance information 2. Change requests 3. Project management plan updates 4. Project documents updates

Project Management Institute, *A Guide to the Project Management Body of Knowledge, (PMBOK® Guide) – Sixth Edition,* Project Management Institute Inc., 2017.

PM Foundation

Definitions

*Project – A temporary endeavor undertaken to create a unique product, service, or result.

*Program – Related projects, subsidiary programs, and program activities that are managed in a coordinated manner to obtain benefits not available from managing them individually.

*Portfolio – Projects, programs, subsidiary portfolios, and operations managed as a group to achieve strategic objectives.

*Progressive Elaboration – The iterative process of increasing the level of detail in a project management plan as greater amounts of information and more accurate estimates become available.

*Project Life Cycle – The series of phases that a project passes through from its start to its completion.

*Project Management Office – An organizational structure that standardizes the project-related governance processes and facilitates the sharing of resources, methodologies, tools and techniques.

Project and Development Life Cycle Types

*Predictive – Also known as waterfall life cycles, the scope, time, and cost are determined as early in the life cycle as possible.

*Iterative – The scope is determined early in the project life cycle, but time and cost estimates are modified as the team's understanding increases.

*Incremental - The deliverable is produced through a series of iterations that successively add functionality within a predetermined time frame.

*Adaptive – Also known as agile or change-driven life cycles. Utilized to respond to high levels of change and increased stakeholder involvement.

*Hybrid – Combination of a predictive and an adaptive life cycle. Known elements follow a predictive life cycle whereas evolving elements follow an adaptive life cycle.

Project Management Office (PMO) Types

Supportive PMO – Low control -- provides templates, lessons learned, and training to the project team -- serves as a project repository.

Controlling PMO – Moderate control -- provides support, implements controls and procedures, and monitors the projects' compliance with the defined framework.

Directive PMO – High control -- directly manages the projects.

*These definitions are taken from the Glossary of the *(PMBOK® Guide) – Sixth Edition*

PM Foundation

Organizational Types

Organic or Simple – Flexible working arrangement with people working side-by-side. PM has little to no authority.

*Functional (Centralized) – A hierarchical organization where each employee has one clear superior, and staff are grouped by areas of specialization and managed by a person with expertise in that area.

Weak Matrix – Matrix that more closely resembles a functional organization. Use of coordinators or expeditors versus project managers.

*Matrix / Balanced Matrix –The project manager shares responsibility with the functional managers for assigning priorities and for directing the work of persons assigned to the project.

Strong Matrix – Matrix that more closely resembles a projectized organization, giving the PM greater authority.

Project-oriented (Composite, hybrid)– Team members grouped by project and the PM has a full time designated role with high authority.

Virtual – Teams are connected by work points or nodes with other members and the PM typically has low to moderate authority, with a full or part-time role.

Multi-divisional – A structure that lacks centralization and the PM has little to no authority and may not have a defined PM role.

Hybrid – A mix of various types of structures where the PM authority and role varies by organization.

Project Roles

*Project Manager – Individual assigned by the performing organization to achieve the project objectives.

*Sponsor – A person or group who provides resources and support for the project, program, or portfolio and is accountable for enabling success.

*Stakeholders – Individuals or organizations that are either involved in the project or are affected by a decision, activity or outcome of the project.

*Seller – A provider or supplier of products, services, or results to an organization

*Project Management Team – The members of the project team who are directly involved in project management activities.

*Project Team – A set of individuals who support the project manager in performing the work of the project to achieve its objectives.

*These definitions are taken from the Glossary of the *(PMBOK® Guide) – Sixth Edition*

Agile Project Management

Agile Manifesto

We are uncovering better ways of developing software by doing it and helping others do it. Through this work we have come to value:

Individuals and interactions over processes and tools
Working software over comprehensive documentation
Customer collaboration over contract negotiation
Responding to change over following a plan

That is, while there is value in the items on the right, we value the items on the left more.

©2001, the Agile Manifesto authors

Key Concepts for Agile Project Management

- Agile project management, also considered adaptive project management, is best suited for high-uncertainty projects with high rates of change, complexity, and risk
- Originated in software development, but application is spreading to other industries
- Approaches typically include:
  - Very short feedback loops
  - Frequent adaptation of process
  - Reprioritization
  - Regularly updated plans
  - Frequent delivery

Popular Agile Approaches

Lean – origin in manufacturing, includes seven principles: eliminate waste, amplify learning, decide as late as possible, deliver as fast as possible, empower, the team, building integrity in, and see the whole

Kanban – includes a visual process management system and an approach to incremental, evolutionary process changes for organization

Scrum – an iterative and incremental software development method used in environments where it is difficult to plan ahead

ScrumBan – minimal documentation/information, uses daily standups but not time-limited sprints

XP – teams perform all software development activities simultaneously

Agile Project Management

Agile Events

Product planning – meeting to determine the vision and roadmap for the project

Sprint planning – prioritizes and plans the work for the next sprint or iteration. Two hours for each week of sprint.

Sprint / iteration – the actual work is completed. Typically ranges from one to four weeks.

Daily stand-up – the daily meeting to exchange status information from the agile team, including: what they did yesterday, what they are doing today, and what do they need assistance with.

Sprint review – a review of the functionality that was built and tested during that sprint or iteration. One hour for each week of sprint.

Sprint retrospective – a meeting with the agile team to review what worked well, what needs improvement, and other key lessons learned. Forty-five minutes for each week of sprint.

Agile Artifacts

Vision – describe the overall vision for the product

Product roadmap – a graphical representation of the product components

Release plan – a graphical representation of the product releases within the roadmap

* Product backlog – an ordered list of user-centric requirements that a team maintains for a product

* Sprint backlog – a list of work items identified by the team to be completed during the sprint

* Burndown chart – a graphical representation of the work remaining versus the time left in a timebox

Velocity

Velocity - the average amount of work a scrum team completes during a sprint, measured in either story points or hours, used to predict how quickly a team can work through the backlog

For example: the product owner wants to complete 500 story points in the backlog. The development team generally completes 50 story points per iteration. The product owner can reasonably assume the team will need ten iterations (give or take) to complete the required work.

*These definitions are taken from the Glossary of the Agile Practice Guide

Project Definitions

PMBOK® Guide - Project and Framework Definitions

* Project life cycle – The phases that the project must go through from the start of the project until the completion of the project. For example: definition, design, development, testing, launch.

* **Project phase** – A group of logically related project tasks or activities that result in a defined output.

* **Phase gate** – A defined process used to validate that the work of the phase has been completed satisfactorily before moving to the next phase.

Project management processes – A set of project activities that cause an end result based on a set of inputs. The PMBOK® Guide framework consists of 49 project management processes.

* **Project management process group** – Groups of related processes. Process groups are not phases. The PMBOK® Guide consists of five process groups:

• Initiating
• Planning
• Executing
• Monitoring and controlling
• Closing

*Project management knowledge area** – Areas of understanding and expertise that may be applied on a particular project based on the defined constraints. The *PMBOK® Guide* consists of ten project management knowledge areas:

• Integration
• Scope
• Schedule
• Cost
• Quality
• Resource
• Communications
• Risk
• Procurement
• Stakeholder

*These definitions are taken from the Glossary of the *(PMBOK® Guide) – Sixth Edition*

PM Power

Types of Power the PM May Leverage

A key and critical skill as a project manager is the ability to effectively navigate the political landscape of the organization, while understanding the culture and environment in which the projects will be performed. There are a number of different types of power that can be used regardless of whether the project manager has positional authority. These approaches aren't "right" or "wrong", rather they need to be applied appropriately with mature judgement based on the circumstances.

Positional – Power that is granted by the organization or an authority. Also known as formal, authoritative or legitimate power. When the project manager is granted authority in the project charter, this is considered positional power.

Informational – The power to gather and disseminate information related to the project.

Referent – Power that comes through individuals respecting the project manager and through the credibility gained by the project manager.

Situational – Power that is gained during a specific or unique situation, such as during an emergency.

Personal or Charismatic – Power granted because the project manager is liked and has an agreeable and pleasant personality.

Relational – Power developed through networking and connections with others in which relationships are cultivated and alliances are created.

Expert – Power that is based on a respect for the expertise and knowledge of the project manager.

Reward-oriented – Power that is generated by the ability to offer something of value to the team members, such as monetary incentives, time off, or praise.

Punitive or Coercive – The power to influence based on fear of punishment or negative consequences.

Ingratiating – Power that is granted based on flattery or platitudes to win favor with the team.

Pressure-based – Power derived from limiting the individuals' freedom of choice to gain compliance to the desired action.

Guilt-based – Power that results from making individuals feel guilty if they do not comply, such as a sense of duty or moral obligation.

Persuasive – Power arrived at by communicating in a manner that compels action from the individuals.

Avoiding – Power that comes from refusing to participate.

13

Common ITTOs

Common Inputs

*Project Management Plan – The document that describes how the project will be executed, monitored and controlled, and closed. The project management plan may be summary level or detailed and includes the project baselines (scope, schedule, cost) and any subsidiary plans.

*Work Performance Data – The raw observations and measurements identified during activities being performed to carry out the project work. Work performance data is an output of Direct and Manage Project Work and is an input to most of the Monitoring & Controlling processes.

Project Documents – A very generic common input that can include any type of project documentation.

*Project Charter – A document issued by the project initiator or sponsor that formally authorizes the existence of a project and provides the PM with the authority to apply organizational resources to project activities.

*Enterprise Environmental Factors (EEF) – Conditions, not under the immediate control of the team, that influence, constrain, or direct the project, program, or durations. Enterprise environmental factors may be internal or external to the organization.

*Organizational Process Assets (OPA) – Plans, processes, policies, procedures, and knowledge bases that are specific to and used by the performing organization. The knowledge bases include lessons learned, past project files, and historical information. On the exam, you can assume you have access to OPAs as a critical input for many of the processes.

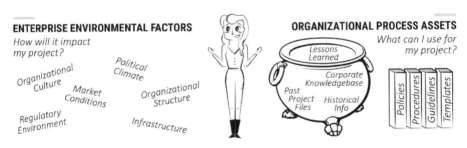

ENTERPRISE ENVIRONMENTAL FACTORS
How will it impact my project?
Organizational Culture
Political Climate
Market Conditions
Organizational Structure
Regulatory Environment
Infrastructure

ORGANIZATIONAL PROCESS ASSETS
What can I use for my project?
Lessons Learned
Corporate Knowledgebase
Past Project Files
Historical Info
Policies
Procedures
Guidelines
Templates

*These definitions are taken from the Glossary of the *(PMBOK® Guide) – Sixth Edition*

Common Tools & Techniques

Expert Judgment – Judgment provided based upon expertise in an application area, knowledge area, discipline, industry, etc., as appropriate for the activity being performed. Such expertise may be provided by any group or person with specialized education, knowledge, skill, experience, or training.

Data Analysis Techniques – Techniques used to organize, assess, and evaluate data and information. Data analysis techniques include:

- Alternatives analysis
- Assessment of other risk parameters
- Assumptions and constraints analysis
- Cost of quality
- Cost benefit analysis
- Decision tree analysis
- Document analysis
- Earned value analysis
- Influence diagrams
- Iteration burndown chart
- Make or buy analysis
- Performance reviews
- Process analysis
- Proposal evaluation

Interpersonal and Team Skills – Skills used to effectively lead and interact with team members and other stakeholders.

- Active listening
- Communication styles assessment
- Conflict management
- Cultural awareness
- Decision making
- Emotional intelligence
- Facilitation
- Influencing
- Leadership
- Meeting management
- Motivation
- Negotiation
- Networking
- Nominal group technique
- Observation / conversation
- Political awareness
- Team building

Data Gathering Techniques – Techniques used to organize, assess, and evaluate data and information. Data gathering techniques include:

- Benchmarking
- Brainstorming
- Check sheets
- Checklists
- Focus groups
- Interviews
- Market research
- Questionnaires and surveys
- Statistical sampling

Decision-Making Techniques – Techniques used to organize, assess, and evaluate data and information. Includes multi-criteria decision analysis and voting.

These definitions are taken from the Glossary of the *(PMBOK® Guide) – Sixth Edition*

Common Tools & Techniques (continued)

*Project Management Information System (PMIS) – An information system consisting of the tools and techniques used to gather, integrate and disseminate the outputs of project management processes.

*Data Representation Techniques – Graphic representations or other methods used to convey data and information.

- Affinity diagrams
- Cause-and-effect diagrams
- Control charts
- Flowcharts
- Hierarchical charts
- Histograms
- Logical data model
- Matrix diagrams

- Matrix-based charts
- Mind mapping
- Probability and impact matrix
- Scatter diagrams
- Stakeholder engagement assessment matrix
- Stakeholder mapping / representation
- Text-oriented formats

Meetings – Interactive communication tool for the exchange of project information.

Common Outputs

Project Management Plan Updates – Updates to the project management plan and/or the components of the project management plan (baselines and subsidiary plans) as modified through the change control process.

Project Documents Updates – Updates to any of the project documentation as a result of progress or project changes.

*Change Requests – A formal proposal to modify a document, deliverable, or baseline. There are five categories of change requests: scope changes, updates, corrective actions, preventive actions, and defect repairs.

Organizational Process Assets Updates – Updated policies, procedures, guidelines, templates, lessons learned, etc.

*Work Performance Information – The analyzed performance data collected from the monitoring and controlling processes. Work performance information is the analysis of the work performance data in comparison with project management plan components, project documents, and other work performance indicators.

Important Sequences

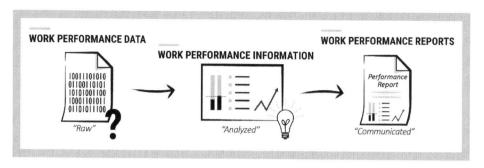

WORK PERFORMANCE DATA

WORK PERFORMANCE INFORMATION

WORK PERFORMANCE REPORTS

Performance Report

"Raw"

"Analyzed"

"Communicated"

DELIVERABLE
Direct & Manage
Project Work

VERIFIED DELIVERABLE
Control Quality

The Healing Touch

ACCEPTED DELIVERABLE
Validate Scope

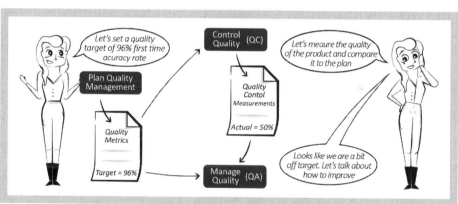

Let's set a quality target of 96% first time acuracy rate

Control Quality (QC)

Let's meaure the quality of the product and compare it to the plan

Plan Quality Management

Quality Contol Measurements

Actual = 50%

Quality Metrics

Manage Quality (QA)

Looks like we are a bit off target. Let's talk about how to improve

Target = 96%

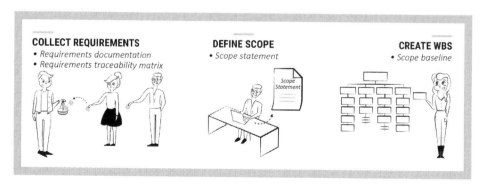

COLLECT REQUIREMENTS
• *Requirements documentation*
• *Requirements traceability matrix*

DEFINE SCOPE
• *Scope statement*

Scope Statement

CREATE WBS
• *Scope baseline*

Integration

Project Charter

- Developed based on information contained within the business case, benefits management plan, and agreement (contract with an external customer)
- Output of the **Develop Project Charter** process
- Formally authorizes the project, demonstrating the organizational commitment to the project and creating a formal record of the project
- Signed by the sponsor and identifies the project manager (if known)

Project Management Plan

- Output of the **Develop Project Management Plan** process
- Ultimate "how-to" guide for the project, defining the basis of the project work and how it will be performed
- Includes all the subsidiary plans. Subsidiary plans provide details around specific areas of the project. For example, the risk management plan details how project risk management will be defined, implemented, controlled, and evaluated for the project.
- Includes the scope, schedule, and cost baselines. Once the project management plan is baselined, any changes would need to occur through the **Perform Integrated Change Control** process.

Deliverables

- Output of the **Direct and Manage Project Work** process
- Any unique and verifiable product or output from the project activities
- Verified deliverables are an output of the **Control Quality** process
- Accepted deliverables are an output of the **Validate Scope** process

Work Performance Data

- Output of the **Direct and Manage Project Work** process
- Raw data, observations and measurements generated by the project
- Becomes a common input to the **Monitor and Control** processes
- Once it is analyzed, it becomes work performance information, a common output

These definitions are taken from the Glossary of the *(PMBOK® Guide) – Sixth Edition*

Integration

Change Control

- Change requests are reviewed through the change control board (CCB).
- Change requests include scope changes, updates, corrective actions, preventive actions, and defect repairs.
- Scope changes are requests for different functionality or other changes to the project scope.
- Updates are changes to formally controlled project documents, plans, etc.
- Corrective actions are reactive requests to attempt to bring the project back into alignment with the project plan, typically related to the schedule or budget.
- Preventive actions are proactive requests to attempt to reverse a negative trend associated with the project plan, typically related to the schedule or budget.
- Defect repairs are requests to correct an error in the quality of a deliverable.

Administrative Closure

Administrative closure of the project or the phase may include the following:

- The actions to satisfy the completion or exit criteria such as updating all documents, confirming delivery and acceptance of the deliverables, ensuring all costs have been charged, personnel have been reassigned, and the final reports have been completed
- The activities related to the completion of the contractual agreements such as, confirming the formal acceptance of the seller's work, finalizing open claims, updating records, and archiving the information
- Collecting project or phase records
- Auditing success or failure
- Managing knowledge sharing and transfer
- Identifying lessons learned
- Archiving project information
- Transferring the product or service to the next phase or production
- Measuring stakeholder satisfaction

These definitions are taken from the Glossary of the *(PMBOK® Guide) – Sixth Edition*

Decision-Making Techniques

Voting – A collective decision-making technique and an assessment process having multiple alternatives with an expected outcome in the form of future actions.

> **Unanimity** – All members agree on a course of action.

> **Majority** – More than half the members agree.

> **Plurality** – The largest subset of the group agrees, even if majority is not achieved.

Autocratic decision making – One individual takes responsibility for making the decision for the group.

Multicriteria decision analysis – A technique that uses a decision matrix to provide a systematic analytical approach for establishing criteria, such as risk levels, uncertainty, and valuation, to evaluate and rank many ideas.

Facilitated Workshops

- Attended by key cross-functional stakeholders
- Primary technique for defining cross-functional requirements
- Fosters relationships, builds trust, and improves communication
- Examples: joint application development or design (JAD) or quality function deployment (QFD) sessions

Decomposition

- Technique for creating the work breakdown structure (WBS)
- Subdivides the project deliverables into smaller, more manageable components
- May be structured by phase, location, or deliverable
- Hierarchical identification numbering is assigned based on the code of accounts / chart of accounts

These definitions are taken from the Glossary of the *(PMBOK® Guide) – Sixth Edition*

Scope

Requirements Documentation

- Describes how the individual requirements will meet the business need for the project
- Must be measurable, testable, traceable, complete, and consistent
- Includes business, stakeholder, solution, transition, project, and quality requirements
- Traceability matrix links requirements from their origin through to the completion of the deliverables

Project Scope Statement

- Describes the project deliverables and the work required to create those deliverables
- Provides a common understanding of the project scope among the stakeholders
- Considered mandatory

WBS

- Graphical, hierarchical depiction of all the project work
- 100% rule: the lower levels roll up to the higher levels, nothing is left out
- Lowest level of a WBS is a work package

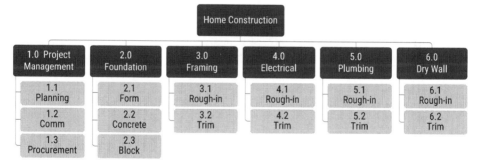

WBS Dictionary

- Companion document to the WBS, providing detailed information on the WBS components

Scope Baseline

- Includes the scope statement, the WBS, and the WBS dictionary
- Component of the project management plan

These definitions are taken from the Glossary of the *(PMBOK® Guide) – Sixth Edition*

Precedence Diagramming Method (PDM)

A project schedule network diagram where the nodes or boxes represent activities and the arrows depict the dependencies. Also called an activity-on-node (AON) diagram.

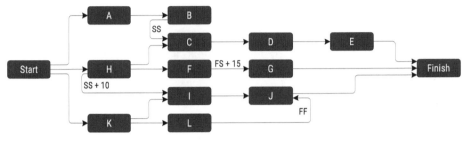

(PMBOK® Guide) - Sixth Edition. Page 193

Precedence Relationships

Finish-to-Start (FS)

Predecessor must finish before successor can start.

Example: The books must be printed before they can be shipped.

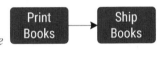

Start-to-Start (SS)

Predecessor must start before successor can start.

Example: As the concrete is being poured, the concrete can be tested

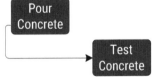

Finish-to-Finish (FF)

Predecessor must finish before successor can finish.

Example: The website must be fully designed and developed before the website quality review can be completed.

Start-to-Finish (SF)

Predecessor must start before successor can finish.

Example: The new nurses shift must start at the hospital before the previous nurse's shift can finish.

Dependency Determination

*Mandatory Dependency – Inherent to the work being done; involves physical limitations, referred to as hard logic.

Example: The books must be printed before they can be shipped.

*Discretionary Dependency – Usually established based on the discretion of the project team, based on best practices or experience, may come from outside sources or industry experts, referred to as preferred logic, preferential logic or soft logic.

Example: The screen shots of the new system are to be approved prior to beginning development of the user guides.

*External Dependency – Involves a relationship between project activities and non–project activities, usually outside of the project team's control.

Example: The city must issue the permits before construction can begin.

Internal Dependency – Involves a relationship between project activities that are within the project team's control.

Example: The team cannot test a software program until it is designed and built.

Lead and Lag

*Lead – Acceleration of a successor activity, only used in a finish-to-start (FS) discretionary relationship. Indicated as a negative number on a network diagram, representing time that is saved.

Example: The photo shoot will take 4 days. The photo editing will take 6 days. Instead of waiting until the end of the 4 day photo shoot to begin editing, we start editing after the first day of shooting. The total duration of the photo shoot and editing is 7 days.

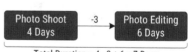

Total Duration = 4 - 3 + 6 = 7 Days

*Lag – Delay of a successor activity, has no resources associated with it, may be used in any type of precedence relationship: FS, SS, FF, SF. Indicated as a positive number on a network diagram, representing time that is added.

Example: Completing the application takes 4 days, once submitted the application takes 5 days to be processed, once approved it takes one day to schedule the exam. The total duration from application to scheduled exam is 10 days.

Total Duration = 4 + 5 + 1 = 10 Days

---

*These definitions are taken from the Glossary of the *(PMBOK® Guide) – Sixth Edition*

Schedule

Effort vs. Duration vs. Elapsed Time

Effort – The number of work units required to complete the activity, referred to as staff-hours, days, or weeks, will need to be identified in order to determine the activity duration.

Duration – The total time to complete the activities based on the resources available, does not include holidays or non-working days, referred to as work days or weeks.

Elapsed Time – The calendar time or span required to complete the activities based on the resources available. Includes holidays and non-working days.

Critical Path Method (CPM)

Calculates the early start and early finish dates and the late start and late finish dates for all schedule activities by performing a forward pass and backward pass analysis through the project schedule network paths. This will determine the critical path: the longest path through the schedule with either zero or negative total float (TF).

ES + DU - 1 = EF		
ES	DU	EF
Activity Name		
LS	TF	LF
LF - DU + 1 = LS		

Forward Pass

Determines the early start (ES) and early finish (EF) dates. ES + duration (DU) - 1 = EF

Backward Pass

Determines the late start (LS) and late finish (LF) dates.

LF - duration (DU) + 1 = LS

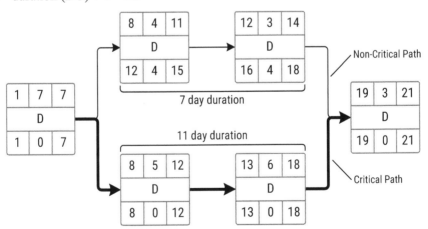

(PMBOK® Guide) – Sixth Edition. Page 211

These definitions are taken from the Glossary of the *(PMBOK® Guide) – Sixth Edition*

Float

Total Float (TF)

- Measured as the difference between the early and late start dates (LS - ES) or the early and late finish dates (LF - EF)

- Shared between the activities in a sequence (a sequence is defined as the activities between a point of path divergence and path convergence)

- Occurs when there are more than one concurrent activities of different durations

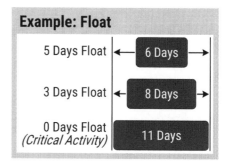

Example: Float

5 Days Float ← 6 Days →

3 Days Float ← 8 Days →

0 Days Float
(*Critical Activity*) | 11 Days

- Represents the amount of time an activity can be delayed without delaying the overall project duration

- Also called float or slack

Free Float (FF)

- Measured by subtracting the EF of the predecessor from the ES of the successor minus 1

- Represents the amount of time that a schedule activity can be delayed without delaying the early start date of any immediate successor activity within the network path

- Only calculated on the last activity in an activity sequence

Schedule Compression Techniques

Fast Tracking

- A technique in which phases or activities that would normally be done sequentially are performed in parallel

- Does not result in increased cost but it does increase the risk

Crashing

- Used if fast-tracking does not save enough time on the schedule

- A technique in which cost and schedule tradeoffs are analyzed to determine how to obtain the greatest amount of compression for the least incremental cost

- Candidate activities are displayed in a crash graph, representing the time saved and the costs increased

These definitions are taken from the Glossary of the *(PMBOK® Guide) – Sixth Edition*

Reserve Analysis

- Evaluates the amount of contingency as compared to the amount of risk remaining on the project
- Budget contingency reserve (contingency) is funding that is allocated for "known-unknowns" (identified risks). Contingency is managed by the project manager and is included in the cost baseline.
- Management reserve, controlled by the project sponsor, is for "unknown-unknowns" (unidentified risks). Management reserve is not included in the cost baseline but is a component of the overall project budget. Management reserve may be used for major scope changes, unidentified or black swan risks, or other circumstances outside of the control of the customer or the project team.

Cost Baseline

- Time-phased budget used as the basis to measure, monitor and control the cost performance, detailing the periodic and cumulative planned value of the work to be completed
- Component of the project management plan
- Typically displayed in an S-curve graph, with the budget at completion (BAC) as the end point. Periodic points of the S-curve graph represent the planned value (PV) of the work to be completed, cumulatively, as of that date.

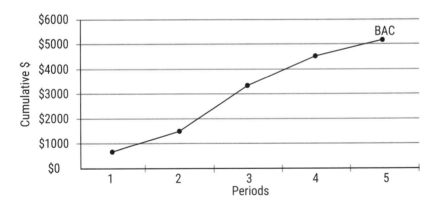

These definitions are taken from the Glossary of the *(PMBOK® Guide) – Sixth Edition*

Cost

Planned Value (PV)

- The dollar value of the work planned to be completed to date
- Cumulative from the start date through the status date

Actual Cost (AC)

- The actual money spent on the project to-date
- Cumulative from the start date through the status date

Earned Value (EV)

- Value earned based on the percentage complete of the budgeted work
- **Earned Value (EV)** = budget at completion (BAC) x % complete
- Percentage complete can either be time-based or effort-based

Earned Value Calculations

- **Schedule Variance (SV)** = earned value - planned value
- **Schedule Performance Index (SPI)** = earned value ÷ planned value
- **Cost Variance (CV)** = earned value - actual cost
- **Cost Performance Index (CPI)** = earned value ÷ actual cost

To-Complete Performance Index (TCPI)

- Efficiency ratio comparing work remaining to money remaining
- Work remaining is calculated as the budget at completion (BAC) minus the earned value (EV)
- Money remaining may be calculated using the budget (BAC) or the forecast (EAC) minus the actual costs (AC)
- TCPI = (BAC-EV) ÷ (BAC-AC)   or   TCPI = (BAC-EV) ÷ (EAC-AC)

Forecasting – Estimate to Complete/Estimate at Completion

- **Estimate to Complete (ETC)** is the estimated remaining costs from this point forward, not including actual costs (AC)
- **Estimate at Completion (EAC)** is the estimated overall project costs at the completion of the project including actual costs (AC)
- There are multiple calculations used to determine the EAC:
- Bottom-up, when there is no variance noted: EAC = estimate to complete (ETC) + actual costs (AC)
- Atypical (one-time) variance: EAC = actual costs (AC) + budget at completion (BAC) - earned value (EV)
- Typical (recurring) variance: EAC = budget at completion (BAC) ÷ cost performance index (CPI)
- EAC calculation considering both SPI and CPI: EAC = AC + ((BAC-EV)/(CPIxSPI))

These definitions are taken from the Glossary of the *(PMBOK® Guide) – Sixth Edition*

Formulas

Term	Formula	Description
Budget at Completion	BAC = total project budget	Assigned project budget
Earned Value	EV = BAC x % complete	Value earned in the work completed
Planned Value	PV = budgeted value of the work to be completed	Assigned value of the work to be completed as of the status date
Schedule Variance	SV = EV - PV	0 = on schedule Negative = behind schedule Positive = ahead of schedule
Schedule Performance Index	SPI = EV ÷ PV	1 = on schedule < 1 = behind schedule > 1 = ahead of schedule
Actual Cost	AC = what has been spent	Actual cost of the work completed as of the status date
Cost Variance	CV = EV - AC	0 = on budget Negative = over budget Positive = under budget
Cost Performance Index	CPI = EV ÷ AC	1 = on budget < 1 = over budget > 1 = under budget
To-Complete Performance Index	TCPI = (BAC-EV) ÷ (BAC-AC) TCPI = (BAC-EV) ÷ (EAC-AC)	Efficiency ratio comparing work remaining (BAC-EV) to money remaining. Money remaining may be based on the budget (BAC) or the forecast (EAC) For TCPI, >1 is bad, reflecting more work than money
Estimate at Completion	EAC = AC + ETC (bottom-up) EAC = AC + BAC – EV (atypical variance) EAC = BAC ÷ CPI (typical variance) EAC = AC + [(BAC – EV) / (CPI x SPI)]	A forecast of the estimated total project spend at completion
Estimate to Complete	ETC = new estimate ETC = EAC - AC	A forecast of the estimated cost remaining to complete the project
Variance at Completion	VAC = BAC - EAC	The difference between the budget and the forecast
Communication Channels	n(n - 1) / 2	The number of communication channels or paths on your project
Three-point Estimate	(O + 4M + P) ÷ 6 (Beta) (O + M + P) ÷ 3 (Triangular)	PERT estimate used for time and/or cost
Lead	Duration A - Lead + Duration B	Acceleration of a successor activity
Lag	Duration A + Lag + Duration B	Delay of a successor activity

(PMBOK® Guide) – Sixth Edition. Page 267

Dump Sheet

Recommended Dump Sheet

As you are preparing for your exam, identify those topics that you may struggle with on the exam. At a minimum, I recommend memorizing the formulas below.

Once seated at your test station write your dump sheet down on the scratch paper provided by the test center. Depending on the leniency of the Prometric location, you may have to wait until after you have completed the system tutorial and started your exam before you can write down your dump sheet. You will receive pencils and a booklet of paper.

EV = BAC x % Complete

SV = EV – PV

SPI = EV ÷ PV

CV = EV – AC

CPI = EV ÷ AC

TCPI = (BAC – EV) ÷ (BAC – AC)

(BAC – EV) ÷ (EAC – AC)

EAC = AC + ETC   (no variance)

EAC = AC + BAC – EV   (atypical variance)

EAC = BAC ÷ CPI   (typical variance)

EAC = AC + [(BAC – EV) / (CPI X SPI)]

ETC = EAC – AC

VAC = BAC – EAC

>0 is Good --- SV and CV and VAC

>1 is Good --- SPI and CPI

>1 is Bad --- TCPI

3-Point / PERT

$$\text{Beta} \quad \frac{O + 4M + P}{6}$$

$$\text{Triangular} \quad \frac{O + M + P}{3}$$

ES + DU – 1 = EF

ES	DU	EF
Activity Name		
LS	TF	LF

LF – DU + 1 = LS

29

Estimating

Analogous Estimating

- Uses a previous similar project as a basis for the current estimate
- Leverages both historical information and expert judgment
- Used in both duration and cost estimating
- Also known as top-down

Example: Last year's website took three months to develop, I estimate that it will take three months to develop a similar website this year

Parametric Estimating

- Uses a statistical relationship between historical data and other variables to determine a unit cost or productivity rate
- Used in both duration and cost estimating

Example: Last week it took me one hour to mow one acre, I estimate that this week it will take me three hours to mow three acres

Three-Point Estimating

- Uses Optimistic, Pessimistic, and Most-likely estimates to calculate a weighted average
- There are two variations: beta or triangular (for the exam, assume beta)
- Used in both duration and cost estimating
- You may see different variations of how these formulas are written:

Beta Distribution

$$\frac{(O+4M+P)}{6} \qquad t_E = \frac{(t_O + 4t_M + t_P)}{6} \qquad c_E = \frac{(c_O + 4c_M + c_P)}{6}$$

Triangular Distribution

$$\frac{(O+M+P)}{3} \qquad t_E = \frac{(t_O + t_M + t_P)}{3} \qquad c_E = \frac{(c_O + c_M + c_P)}{3}$$

t = time   c = cost

Example: With 6 resources it will take 5 days (optimistic), if it is just me it will take 15 days (pessimistic), and if I have 3 resources and it will take 7 days (most likely)

(5 + (4x7) + 15) / 6 = 8 days

These definitions are taken from the Glossary of the *(PMBOK® Guide) – Sixth Edition*

Plan Quality Management

- Determines the quality standards for the project and product
- Creates the quality management plan, process improvement plan, and the quality metrics

Control Quality (QC)

- Evaluates the products or outputs to ensure that they comply with the requirements
- Creates the QC measurements, verified deliverables, and validated changes

Manage Quality (QA)

- Translates the quality plan into executable quality activities.
- Increases the probability of achieving quality objectives
- A component of the **Manage Quality** process is conducting quality assurance
- QA audits the results from QC (the QC measurements) against the quality metrics to identify areas for improvement
- Considered the umbrella over continuous process improvement
- Managing quality activities are considered a cost of conformance (money spent to avoid failures)

Quality Approaches

- **Deming** – Organizations can increase quality and reduce costs by practicing continuous process improvement and by thinking of manufacturing as a system, not bits and pieces.
- **Juran** – Applied the Pareto principle to quality issues (80% of the problems originate from 20% of the causes) and also developed "Juran's Trilogy": quality planning, quality control, and quality improvement.
- **Crosby** – Created the principle of Doing it Right the First Time (DIRFT).
- **Shewhart** – Developed the Plan-Do-Check-Act (PDCA) Cycle.

These definitions are taken from the Glossary of the *(PMBOK® Guide) – Sixth Edition*

Quality

Quality Terms

*Quality – The degree to which characteristics fulfill requirements.

*Grade – A category assigned to products or services having the same functional use but different technical characteristics.

*Precision – The values of repeated measurement are consistent.

*Accuracy – The measured value is very close to the target value.

*Attribute Sampling – The result conforms, or it does not.

Variable Sampling – The result is rated on a scale that measures the degree of conformity.

Special Causes of Variance – Unusual events, difficult to predict.

Common Causes of Variance – Normal process variation (aka random causes)

*Tolerances – The result is acceptable if it falls within the range specified by the tolerance.

*Control Limits – The process is in control if the result falls within the control limits.

Quality Concepts

*Customer Satisfaction – Satisfaction is achieved through understanding, evaluating, defining, and managing expectations.

Continuous Improvement – The PDCA cycle is the basis for quality improvement; quality initiatives should improve the quality of the project's management as well as the quality of the project's product.

Prevention Over Inspection – Quality should be built into the products, not inspected in; prevention is proactive versus inspection which is reactive.

Mutually Beneficial Partnership with Suppliers – Managing the relationship with the focus on long-term relationships versus short term gains.

Management Responsibility – Quality requires the participation of all team members, but it is management's responsibility to provide the appropriate tools required to deliver quality.

*These definitions are taken from the Glossary of the *(PMBOK® Guide) – Sixth Edition*

Quality Tools

Ishikawa / Fishbone / Cause & Effect

The problem statement at the head of the fishbone is the starting point to trace the source of the problem back to its root cause.

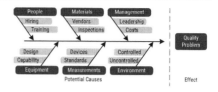

Control Chart

Plots quality results in terms of control limits to determine stability; upper and lower specification limits reflect the maximum and minimum values allowed.

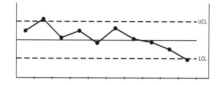

Flowchart

Maps a process, showing activities, decision points, etc, in order to help the team anticipate quality problems and where they may occur.

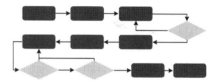

Histogram

Bar chart that shows a distribution of variables, where the height of the bar represents the frequency of occurring.

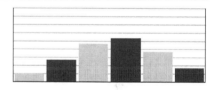

Affinity Diagram

Organizes potential causes of defects into groups showing areas that should be prioritized

Scatter Diagram / Correlation Chart

Shows the pattern of relationship between two variables. Uses a regression line to explain or predict how the change in an independent variable will change a dependent variable.

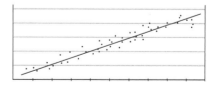

These definitions are taken from the Glossary of the *(PMBOK® Guide) – Sixth Edition*

Conflict Management Approaches

Compromising / Reconciling – Implies that one or both parties give up some of their interests in order to come to an agreement -- may be seen as a "lose–lose".

Used when the individuals are not able to reach consensus.

Collaborating / Problem Solving – Treating conflict as a problem to be solved by examining alternatives; requires a give-and-take attitude and open dialogue; the best way to manage conflict from the *PMBOK® Guide* perspective.

Used when the team is working well together, has a cooperative attitude and open dialogue.

Forcing / Direct – One person forces a solution on another.

Used when the scenarios involve legal, safety, or ethical concerns.

Smoothing / Accommodating – A temporary way to solve a problem; focuses on common ground between the individuals and neutralizing the emotion.

Used when the individuals are in a state of heightened emotion that is preventing them from reaching agreement.

Withdrawing / Avoiding – Removing yourself from the conflict.

Used when the conflict does not impact the project objectives and is not a legal, safety or ethical issue.

(PMBOK® Guide) – Sixth Edition. Page 394

Stages of Team Development – Tuckman's Ladder

Forming – Begins when the team meets and learns about the project, their roles and responsibilities -- at this point, the team members are isolated and not as open with each other.

Storming – The team begins to address the project work, technical decisions, and the project management approach -- the environment can become destructive if the team members are not working collaboratively or are not open to differing ideas and perspectives.

Norming – Team members begin to work together and adjust work habits and behaviors to support the team, increasing their trust.

Performing – For teams that reach the performing stage, they are a well-organized team and are interdependent, working through issues smoothly and effectively.

Adjourning – The team completes the work and moves on to other activities.

(PMBOK® Guide) – Sixth Edition. Page 328

Organizational and Motivational Theorists

Maslow's Hierarchy of Needs

Lower level needs must be met before higher level needs are considered. Often depicted as a pyramid with 5 levels: physiological, safety, social, self-esteem, self-actualization.

Herzberg's Two-Factor Theory

Motivators – Give positive satisfaction, arising from intrinsic conditions of the job itself, such as recognition, achievement, or personal growth.

Hygiene factors – Do not give positive satisfaction, although dissatisfaction results from their absence. These are extrinsic to the work itself and include aspects such as company policies, supervisory practices, or salary.

Vroom's Expectancy Theory

Predicts that employees in an organization will be motivated when they believe that putting in more effort will yield rewards. Vroom's theory assumes that behavior results from conscious choices among alternatives whose purpose it is to maximize pleasure and to minimize pain.

McGregor's Theory of X and Y

'**X**' **theory** states that people are generally lazy, do not want to work and thus need to be micromanaged.

'**Y**' **theory** states that people are self-led and motivated and can accomplish things on their own with little intervention. McGregor believed that people can fall into either category.

Ouchie's Theory Z

Organizations can increase employee loyalty by providing a job for life with a strong focus on the well–being of the employees.

McClelland's Achievement Theory

Need for achievement (N-Ach) is an individual's desire for significant accomplishment.

Those with low N-Ach may choose very easy tasks, in order to minimize risk of failure, or highly difficult tasks, such that a failure would not be embarrassing.

Those with high N-Ach tend to choose moderately difficult tasks, feeling that they are challenging, but within reach.

Communication

Communication Model

The general communication model highlights the key components: encoding and decoding of the message, the message itself, medium, and noise or distractions.

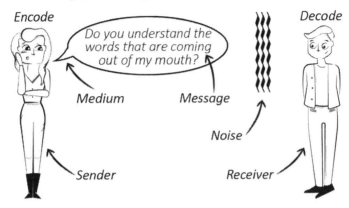

Do you understand the words that are coming out of my mouth?

Encode

Decode

Medium

Message

Noise

Sender

Receiver

(PMBOK® Guide) – Sixth Edition. Page 373

Communication Methods

Interactive Communication – The most efficient method to ensure a common understanding as it is real time, such as meetings or video conferences.

Push Communication – Delivered by the sender to the recipients. While it can be confirmed that it was sent, it does not necessarily mean it was received and understood, such as e-mail or voicemail.

Pull Communication – Provides access to the information however the receiver must proactively retrieve it, such as from a bulletin board or repository.

(PMBOK® Guide) – Sixth Edition. Page 374

5Cs of Written Communication

1. Correct grammar and spelling
2. Concise expression and elimination of excess words
3. Clear purpose and expression directed to the needs of the reader
4. Coherent logical flow of ideas
5. Controlling flow of words and ideas

(PMBOK® Guide) – Sixth Edition. Page 363

Risk

Risk Terms

Individual Project Risk – An uncertain event that if it occurs will have an impact on the project.

Opportunity – A positive project risk.

Threat – A negative project risk.

Trigger – Indicates that a risk has occurred or is about to occur.

Contingent Response Strategy – Planned in advance but only used when the risk event or the trigger occurs.

Fallback Plan – Used when the primary response is inadequate.

Residual Risks – Risks that remain after planned responses have been taken.

Secondary Risks – Arise as an outcome of implementing a risk response.

Workaround – A response to a negative risk that is not planned in advance.

Issue – A realized negative risk.

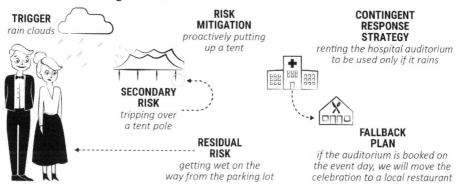

TRIGGER
rain clouds

RISK MITIGATION
proactively putting up a tent

CONTINGENT RESPONSE STRATEGY
renting the hospital auditorium to be used only if it rains

SECONDARY RISK
tripping over a tent pole

RESIDUAL RISK
getting wet on the way from the parking lot

FALLBACK PLAN
if the auditorium is booked on the event day, we will move the celebration to a local restaurant

Risk Identification

- Begins very early in the project (presumably before chartering).
- Must involve other people: SMEs, stakeholders, team members, consultants, PMO.
- Is ongoing throughout the project.

Qualitative Risk Analysis

- Prioritizes identified risks for further action by assessing and combining their probability of occurring and the impact on the project objectives if they do occur.
- Often leverages a probability and impact matrix to evaluate the project risks.
- All risks are evaluated through qualitative risk analysis.
- This process is a relatively quick and easy way to establish priorities for managing risk and determining the appropriate risk response.

These definitions are taken from the Glossary of the *(PMBOK® Guide) – Sixth Edition*

Risk

Quantitative Risk Analysis

- Evaluates the aggregate effect of the risks on the project objectives
- Assigns a numerical/quantitative, rating, reflecting impact to the budget and/or schedule

Probability Distributions

- Represent the impact of the uncertainty on the budget and/or schedule
- Continuous distributions represent the data produced by risk modeling and simulation
- Discrete distributions represent uncertain events and may be depicted in either beta or triangular distributions
- Uniform distributions are used when there is no obvious value that is more likely than any other

Sensitivity Analysis

- Determines which risks have the most potential impact on the project
- For example, a tornado diagram, as depicted here, displays cost risk data by range of potential impact

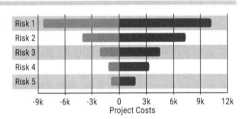

Decision Tree Analysis

- A diagram that depicts a decision under consideration
- Displays the implications of available alternatives

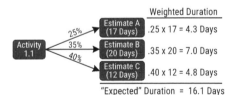

Expected Monetary Value (EMV) Analysis

- Calculates the average outcome when the future includes scenarios that may or may not happen
- Calculated by multiplying the value of each possible outcome by its probability of occurrence, and adding them together for each branch of the tree

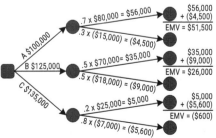

Figures adapted from the *(PMBOK® Guide) – Sixth Edition.* Page 434, 435

These definitions are taken from the Glossary of the *(PMBOK® Guide) – Sixth Edition*

Risk

Risk Response Planning

- Prioritized risks are evaluated for an appropriate response
- Risk owner is assigned to the risk
- Funding, if needed, will be allocated
- Planned risk responses should be appropriate to the level and priority of the risk, while realistic within the context of the project

Strategies for Negative Risks (Threats)

Avoid – Changing the project management plan to eliminate the threat posed by an adverse risk.

Transfer – Shifting the negative impact to a third party.

Escalate – Provide the risk information to a senior party for resolution.

Mitigate – Reducing the probability and/or impact of an adverse risk event to an acceptable level.

Accept – Acknowledging the risk but not taking a proactive response. Active acceptance establishes a contingent response strategy, passive acceptance takes no action.

(PMBOK® Guide) – Sixth Edition. Page 442

Strategies for Positive Risks (Opportunities)

Exploit – Making the opportunity definitely happen through identifying strategies to eliminate the uncertainty.

Share – Allocating ownership to a third party who is best able to capture the opportunity for the benefit of the project.

Escalate – Providing the risk information to a senior party for investigation

Enhance – Modifying the size of the opportunity by increasing the probability and/or positive impacts.

Accept – Willing to take advantage of an opportunity if it comes along, but not changing the plan to actively pursue it.

(PMBOK® Guide) – Sixth Edition. Page 444

Comparison of Strategies

Threats / Opportunities

Avoid .....is to..... Exploit
Transfer .....is to..... Share
Escalate .....is to..... Escalate
Mitigate .....is to..... Enhance
Accept .....is to..... Accept

Fixed Price Contracts (risk to seller)

Firm Fixed Price (FFP)
Fixed total price; most common contract type; any cost increase is the responsibility of the seller.

Fixed Price Incentive Fee (FPIF)
Fixed price plus financial incentives tied to achieving agreed-to metrics.

Fixed Price with Economic Price Adjustments (FP–EPA)
Fixed price with a special provision for inflation or cost increases; typically used for longer term contracts.

Cost Reimbursable Contracts (risk to buyer)

Cost Plus Fixed Fee (CPFF)
Seller is reimbursed for allowable costs and also receives a fixed fee calculated as a percentage of the initial estimated project costs.

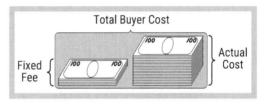

Cost Plus Incentive Fee (CPIF)
Seller is reimbursed for allowable costs and receives an incentive fee for achieving performance objectives; if final costs are less or more than the original estimate, the buyer & seller share the difference based on a pre-negotiated split.

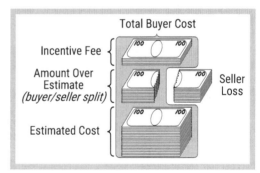

Cost Plus Award Fee (CPAF)
Seller is reimbursed for costs, but the majority of the fee is earned based on broad subjective performance criteria.

Time and Material Contracts (T&M) (moderate risk to buyer)

A hybrid type of contractual agreement that has both cost-reimbursable and fixed-price type arrangements. T&M contracts are usually used for staff augmentation, acquisition of experts and any outside support.

T&M contracts can increase in contract value as if they were cost-reimbursable contracts and as such, the organization may add a "not-to-exceed" value to prevent unlimited cost growth.

These definitions are taken from the Glossary of the *(PMBOK® Guide) – Sixth Edition*

Stakeholder Analysis

- Identifies all project stakeholders and their roles, departments, interests, knowledge levels, expectations, and level of influence
- Identifies the potential impact or support expected from each stakeholder

Power / Interest Grid

Classifies stakeholders based on their level of authority (power) and their level of concern (how likely they are to show interest).

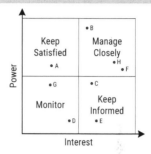

Power / Influence grid

Classifies stakeholders based on their level of authority (power) and their active involvement (influence).

Influence / Impact grid

Classifies stakeholders based on their active involvement (influence) and their ability to effect changes to the project (impact).

Salience Model

Classifies stakeholders based on their power (ability to impose their will), urgency (need for immediate attention), and legitimacy (involvement is appropriate).

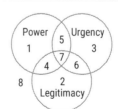

1. Dormant
2. Discretionary
3. Demanding
4. Dominant
5. Dangerous
6. Dependent
7. Definitive
8. Non Stakeholder

Professional and Social Responsibility

Code of Ethics and Professional Conduct

Applies to:

- All PMI® Members
- Non-members who hold a PMI® certification
- Non-members who apply to commence a PMI® certification process
- Non-members who serve PMI® in a volunteer capacity

Aspirational Standards of Conduct – The conduct we strive to uphold as practitioners. Although they may be difficult to measure, these standards are an expectation and are not optional.

Mandatory Standards of Conduct – Establish firm requirements and those who do not conduct themselves in accordance will be subject to disciplinary action before the PMI® Ethics Review Committee.

Code Values

Responsibility – Our duty to take ownership for the decisions we make or fail to make, the actions we take or fail to take, and the consequences that result.

Respect – Our duty to show a high regard for ourselves, others, and the resources entrusted to us. Resources entrusted to us may include people, money, reputation, the safety of others, and natural or environmental resources.

Fairness – Our duty to make decisions and act impartially and objectively. Our conduct must be free from competing self-interest, prejudice and favoritism.

Honesty – Our duty to understand the truth and act in a truthful manner both in our communications and in our conduct.

Adapted from the PMI® Code of Ethics, PMI.org

Professional and Social Responsibility

Code Definitions

Abusive Manner – Conduct that results in physical harm or creates intense feelings of fear, humiliation, manipulation, or exploitation in another person.

Conflict of Interest – A situation that arises when a practitioner of project management is faced with making a decision or doing some act that will benefit the practitioner or another person or organization to which the practitioner owes a duty of loyalty and at the same time will harm another person or organization to which the practitioner owes a similar duty of loyalty.

Duty of Loyalty – A person's responsibility, legal or moral, to promote the best interest of an organization or other person with whom they are affiliated.

Practitioner – A person engaged in an activity that contributes to the management of a project, portfolio, or program, as part of the project management profession.

Other Responsibilities

Maintaining individual integrity – Being truthful, protecting confidential information, reporting violations of ethics and laws, not receiving or giving inappropriate gifts, following copyright laws.

Contributing to the project management knowledge base – Sharing of lessons learned, documenting and writing articles or conducting research on project management practices, mentoring other project professionals, and supporting the ongoing project education of team members and stakeholders.

Enhancing your personal professional competence – Identification of your strengths and weaknesses and planning your professional development activities accordingly.

Promoting interaction and open communication among stakeholders – Balancing stakeholders' interests throughout the life of the project.

Adapted from the PMI® Code of Ethics, PMI.org

Integration Processes

Develop Project Charter (*PMBOK® Guide* pg 75)

Secures authorization for the project to begin, creating the project charter.

Key Outputs: Project charter | Assumption log

Develop Project Management Plan (*PMBOK® Guide* pg 82)

Documents how the project is going to be executed, monitored and controlled and closed. Incorporates all the subsidiary plans and the project baselines into the project management plan.

Key Output: Project management plan

Direct and Manage Project Work (*PMBOK® Guide* pg 90)

Performs the work defined in the project management plan to achieve the project's objectives.

Key Outputs: Deliverables | Work performance data | Issue log

Manage Project Knowledge (*PMBOK® Guide* pg 98)

Uses existing knowledge and creates new knowledge to achieve the project's objectives and contribute to organizational learning.

Key Output: Lessons learned register

Monitor and Control Project Work (*PMBOK® Guide* pg 105)

Tracks, reviews, and regulates the project to meet the performance objectives defined in the project management plan.

Key Output: Work performance reports

Perform Integrated Change Control (*PMBOK® Guide* pg 113)

Reviews all change requests, approves and manages changes to the deliverables, organizational process assets, project documents, and the project management plan.

Key Output: Approved change requests

Close Project or Phase (*PMBOK® Guide* pg 121)

Finalizes all activities across all the project management process groups to formally complete the project or phase.

Key Outputs: Final product, service or result transition | Final report

Plan Scope Management (*PMBOK® Guide* pg 134)

Creates the scope management plan, documenting how the project scope will be defined, validated, and controlled.

Key Outputs: Scope management plan | Requirements management plan

Collect Requirements (*PMBOK® Guide* pg 138)

Documents stakeholder requirements for both the project and the product.

Key Outputs: Requirements documentation | Requirements traceability matrix

Define Scope (*PMBOK® Guide* pg 150)

Develops a detailed written description of the project and product.

Key Output: Project scope statement

Create WBS (*PMBOK® Guide* pg 156)

Subdivides project deliverables and project work into smaller work packages.

Key Output: Scope baseline (WBS, WBS dictionary, scope statement)

Validate Scope (*PMBOK® Guide* pg 165)

Obtains final customer or end-user acceptance of the completed project deliverables.

Key Output: Accepted deliverables

Control Scope (*PMBOK® Guide* pg 167)

Identifies any variances between the scope baseline and the work being completed on the project.

Plan Schedule Management (*PMBOK® Guide* pg 179)

Establishes the guidelines for how the project schedule will be planned, developed, managed, executed, and controlled.

Key Output: Schedule management plan

Define Activities (*PMBOK® Guide* pg 183)

Decomposes the work packages from the WBS into schedule activities.

Key Outputs: Activity list | Activity attributes | Milestone list

Sequence Activities (*PMBOK® Guide* pg 187)

Identifies relationships that exist between the activities and documents those relationships in a schedule network diagram.

Key Output: Project schedule network diagrams

Estimate Activity Durations (*PMBOK® Guide* pg 195)

Determines the level of effort and the duration for each activity.

Key Outputs: Duration estimates | Basis of estimates

Develop Schedule (*PMBOK® Guide* pg 205)

Documents all time planning process outputs into the project schedule.

Key Outputs: Schedule baseline | Project schedule | Schedule data | Project calendars

Control Schedule (*PMBOK® Guide* pg 222)

Identifies the variance between the schedule baseline and actual project progress.

Key Output: Schedule forecasts

Cost / Quality Processes

Plan Cost Management (*PMBOK® Guide* pg 235)

Establishes the guidelines for how the project costs will be planned, developed, managed, executed, and controlled.

Key Output: Cost management plan

Estimate Costs (*PMBOK® Guide* pg 240)

Determines cost estimates for the project activities.

Key Outputs: Cost estimates | Basis of estimates

Determine Budget (*PMBOK® Guide* pg 248)

Estimates the timing of the project costs across the life of the project in order to develop the cost performance baseline and determine the funding requirements.

Key Outputs: Cost baseline | Project funding requirements

Control Costs (*PMBOK® Guide* pg 257)

Identifies the variance between the baseline and actual costs, determining project forecasts.

Key Output: Cost forecasts

Plan Quality Management (*PMBOK® Guide* pg 277)

Identifies the quality standards for the project and the product, documenting how the project will demonstrate compliance with those quality requirements.

Key Outputs: Quality management plan | Quality metrics

Manage Quality (*PMBOK® Guide* pg 288)

Audits the quality requirements and the results from quality control to ensure the project is employing the appropriate processes to achieve the project quality objectives.

Key Outputs: Quality reports | Test and evaluation documents

Control Quality (*PMBOK® Guide* pg 298)

Validates that the project outputs and deliverables are achieving the quality metrics, validates that approved change requests are implemented appropriately.

Key Outputs: Quality control measurements | Verified deliverables

Resource Processes

Plan Resource Management (*PMBOK® Guide* pg 312)

Develops the human resource plan and documents the project resource roles, responsibilities, and reporting relationships. Also creates the staffing management plan.

Key Outputs: Resource management plan | Team charter

Estimate Activity Resources (*PMBOK® Guide* pg 322)

Determines the type and quantities of material, people, equipment or supplies required to perform each activity.

Key Outputs: Resource requirements | Basis of estimates | Resource breakdown structure

Acquire Resources (*PMBOK® Guide* pg 328)

Confirms resource availability and obtains the team necessary to complete project assignments.

Key Outputs: Physical resource assignments | Project team assignments | Resource calendars

Develop Team (*PMBOK® Guide* pg 336)

Improves the competencies, team interaction, and the overall team environment to enhance project performance.

Key Output: Team performance assessments

Manage Team (*PMBOK® Guide* pg 345)

Tracks team member performance, provides feedback, resolves issues, and manages changes to optimize project performance.

Control Resources (*PMBOK® Guide* pg 352)

Ensures that the physical resources assigned and allocated to the project are available as planned, as well as monitoring the planned versus actual utilization of resources and taking corrective action as necessary.

Communication Processes

Plan Communications Management (*PMBOK® Guide* pg 366)

Creates the communication plan, detailing the stakeholders' communication needs and the frequency, format, and content of the project communications.

Key Output: Communication management plan

Manage Communications (*PMBOK® Guide* pg 379)

Manages communication in order to satisfy the needs of, and resolve issues with, project stakeholders.

Key Output: Project communications

Monitor Communications (*PMBOK® Guide* pg 388)

Provides the current status of the project progress against the baselines to the stakeholders, including variance information and project forecasting.

Risk Processes

Plan Risk Management (*PMBOK® Guide* pg 401)

Determines the project approach to risk management.

Key Output: Risk management plan

Identify Risks (*PMBOK® Guide* pg 409)

Identifies the risks (both negative and positive) that affect the project and documents the risk characteristics.

Key Outputs: Risk register | Risk report

Perform Qualitative Risk Analysis (*PMBOK® Guide* pg 419)

Prioritizes the risks for further action by determining the probability of risk occurrence and the impact on the project objectives should the risk occur.

Perform Quantitative Risk Analysis (*PMBOK® Guide* pg 428)

Evaluates the project risks using techniques such as simulation and modeling to provide a numerical and probabilistic analysis of the risks and the project.

Plan Risk Responses (*PMBOK® Guide* pg 437)

Determines the appropriate risk responses for the identified risks.

Implement Risk Responses (*PMBOK® Guide* pg 449)

Implements agreed-upon risk response plans, ensuring that risk responses are executed as planned.

Monitor Risks (*PMBOK® Guide* pg 453)

Monitors the project risk environment and audits the effectiveness of risk responses.

Procurement / Stakeholder Processes

Plan Procurement Management (*PMBOK® Guide* pg 466)

Documents project purchasing decisions, specifying the approach and identifying potential sellers.

Key Outputs: Procurement management plan | Procurement strategy | Bid documents | Procurement statement of work | Source selection criteria | Make-or-buy decisions | Independent cost estimates

Conduct Procurements (*PMBOK® Guide* pg 482)

Obtains seller responses, selects a seller, and awards the contract.

Key Outputs: Selected sellers | Agreements

Control Procurements (*PMBOK® Guide* pg 492)

Manages the relationship with the vendors, ensuring that the contract terms and conditions are being met.

Key Outputs: Closed procurements | Procurement documentation updates

Identify Stakeholders (*PMBOK® Guide* pg 507)

Identifies the project stakeholders and prioritizes the project manager's communications and efforts based upon a stakeholder analysis (such as power/interest).

Key Output: Stakeholder register

Plan Stakeholder Engagement (*PMBOK® Guide* pg 516)

Develops appropriate management strategies to engage stakeholders throughout the project, based on their needs, interests, and potential impact on project success.

Key Output: Stakeholder engagement plan

Manage Stakeholder Engagement (*PMBOK® Guide* pg 523)

Communicating and working with stakeholders to meet their needs and expectations throughout the project.

Monitor Stakeholder Engagement (*PMBOK® Guide* pg 530)

Continual process of controlling stakeholder engagement as defined in the stakeholder management plan.

Qualifications

In order to qualify to complete the Project Management Professional (PMP)® exam, professional project managers must meet the following criteria:

Education:

- 35 hours of project management education prior to submitting the application.

Experience:

- With a bachelor's degree or higher, 4500 hours and 36 months of project management experience in a professional capacity within the past eight years.
- Without a bachelor's degree, 7500 hours and 60 months of project management experience in a professional capacity within the past eight years.

Application Timeline

Step	Process	Approximate Time
1	Review the certification requirements, verify your eligibility, and create an account on pmi.org.	1 day
2	Organize and document your project experience. I recommend using PM Learning Solution's *PMP® Application Assistant Spreadsheet* (PMLearningSolutions.com/PMP-spreadsheet).	3 days
3	Using PMLS's *PMP® Application Assistant Spreadsheet* as a reference, complete the on-line PMP® application at pmi.org and submit. Upon submission you will be notified if you were selected for the random audit (approximately 25% of applications are selected).	Immediate
4	If you are audited, complete all audit forms and mail them to PMI®. Within 5 to 10 days you will receive an e-mail saying either: • Here is your test code and scheduling instructions • You have failed to meet the audit requirements. Please refer to the PMP® Handbook for our refund policy procedure.	5-10 days
5	In five business days you will receive an e-mail with one of three responses: • Your application is approved. Please pay your exam fees. • Your application does not appear to meet the requirements. Please address and re-submit. • Sorry, you have failed to meet the requirements. Your application has been denied.	5 days
6	Log into pmi.org and pay your exam fee. Within minutes you will receive a confirmation e-mail with your test code and your scheduling instructions.	Immediate
7	When you have your test code, access prometric.com/pmi to schedule your exam	1-2 weeks

Question-Oriented Tips

- There are certain questions that contain extra information. This information is irrelevant and it does not relate to the correct answer. Beware of such questions and remember it isn't necessary to use all the information provided to answer the question.
- Each question has only one correct answer. You need to select the most appropriate answer. Beware of choices that represent true statements but are not relevant. Be sure to read all the options before you select any one.
- You need to answer the questions from a PMI® perspective -- not from your own perspective, which you acquired through experience. Remember that PMI® is trying to present an ideal environment for project managers which may be different from your own experience.
- Beware of answer choices that represent generalizations, which may be characterized by words such as always, never, must, or completely; these are often the incorrect choices.
- Look out for choices that represent special cases. These choices tend to be correct and are characterized by words such as often, sometimes, may, generally, and perhaps.
- The correct answer may not be grammatically correct.

PMI® Concept-Oriented Tips

- The project manager takes an active approach to the job by not waiting until a risk materializes and becomes a problem. This is an extremely important concept that might affect many questions on an exam. The project manager does not escalate problems to upper management or to the customer before fully analyzing them and identifying options.
- When answering a question related to what the project manager should do in a specific situation, you should rephrase the question to: What is the first thing the project manager will do given such a situation and given his or her proactive nature?
- Assume that lessons learned and historical databases are available. This might not be true in a real-life situation.
- Roles and responsibilities need to be properly defined.

General Tips

- Practice eliminating the completely implausible options first.
- There is no penalty for guessing; thus, do not leave any question blank.
- There will always be those situations where you have no idea what the question is asking. Use educated guessing to select the most appropriate option. Remember, you only have an average of 72 seconds for each question. If you do not know the answer of a question, mark it and move on and revisit it later if you have time.
- Answer the questions based on the *PMBOK® Guide* concepts first, and then consider your experience. If they are in conflict, the *PMBOK® Guide* wins.

Exam Day Experience

- Verify the location of your test center, anticipate driving conditions (such as rush-hour traffic), and plan to arrive at least 30 minutes early. You will need to show ID and your name on your picture ID must match your PMI® application.

- All your belongings, including your cell phone and possibly your watch, will need to be put into a locker. The key to the locker will remain in your possession throughout the exam.

- If you feel you will need a snack or a drink during testing, be sure to leave them on the designated shelf in the testing center lobby. No food, drink, or gum is allowed in the testing room. If you put it in your locker, you will not be able to access it during the test.

- Use the restroom prior to starting your test. If you need to use the restroom during your exam, your exam clock will continue to run.

- When you are called to go back to the testing room, you will need to reverse your pockets (if possible), roll up your sleeves, and possibly be checked with a metal detecting wand. Do not take offense to these actions, as they are meant to protect the credibility of the exam and the testing process.

- For the Certified Associate in Project Management (CAPM)® exam, you will be provided with two dry-erase sheets and a pen. For the PMP® exam, you will be provided with a booklet of paper and multiple pencils. We are hearing that some sites are also using the dry-erase sheets for the PMP® exam versus the paper booklet. Some test centers will offer you a calculator, others may not. If they do not give you one, ask. They may refuse and have you use the one in the testing mechanism itself.

- The proctor will escort you to your computer. There will be a camera on the room, and possibly one over your computer station. If you are worried about noise/distraction, they have headphones available. Some centers will allow you to bring in headphones, as well.

- When you sit down at your computer, you will first need to acknowledge your name on the screen. You will then have fifteen minutes to complete the tutorial, which should only take you a few minutes. In the past, you were able to complete your "memorized" dump sheet during this time allocation. Unfortunately, PMI and Prometric have changed the rules on this and you are not permitted to write down your dump sheet until your actual exam time starts.

- Once you begin the test, the question-counter will appear in one corner of the screen and the timer in the other corner.

- If you need to take a break for a drink, snack or to use the restroom, your clock will continue to run on your exam. You will need to sign out of the room and back in to the room. You will not be allowed access to your locker.

- For each question, you have the option to answer the question, answer the question and mark it for review, or simply leave it blank. You can navigate forward and backward through the questions. PMI has also enhanced the exam functionality by allowing users to strike-through answers that they want to eliminate and by adding a highlight feature to the question text.

- After the last question, you will have a summary screen showing the questions answered and those that are marked or left blank. You will have the option of reviewing all or reviewing just those that are blank and marked.

- Once you have completed the exam, there will be a pop-up confirming you are ready to submit.

- Upon submission, you will first receive a survey and then you will receive the results of your exam on the screen. Acknowledge your results on the screen and then see the proctor for your printed report.

7 Deadly Sins of PMP® Exam Prep

In order to pass on your first attempt, be aware of these common mistakes made by people who fail the exam:

1. They **only read the *PMBOK® Guide*** or otherwise fail to properly prepare and understand how all of the concepts work together. The PMP® exam is much more than just definitions and processes. It requires a full understanding of how the concepts work together in practice.

2. They assume that **years of project management experience** and/or the **ability to "test well"** will get the job done on the exam. Because the PMP® exam tests your ability to apply *PMBOK® Guide* processes to practical situations, many aspirants find that the questions do not necessarily parallel their experience. In addition, the PMP® test is not a test you can "logic" your way through, even if you do test well.

3. They struggle with **exam anxiety**. As one of the most common fears, exam anxiety propels the tester into fight-or-flight mode which can significantly impair their ability to understand the questions. Recognizing your anxiety and the signs of escalation and having go-to strategies are highly recommended.

4. They **over-analyze, over-read the questions**, consuming too much time. We are project managers and, as such, we are typically analytical. We tend to add more to a question based on our experience. This can seriously derail progress during the 4-hour exam.

5. They **change their answers** after reviewing the questions. Usually your gut is right. If you have extra time during the exam, do not review all of your questions. I recommend reviewing math questions mainly – it never hurts to run your numbers again. But revisiting all questions, can lead to changing answers. The first answer selected is typically the right answer.

6. They **do not have a memorized "dump sheet"**. Think of your dump sheet as your security blanket. At a minimum it will contain all of your earned value, forecasting, and TCPI formulas. This is not stuff you want to stress about remembering during the exam.

7. They **rush through the exam.** Sometimes it is because people get bored and check-out after a few hours. Sometimes it is because they are stressed about time. Being successful on the exam requires you to balance taking too much time with taking too little time.

Maintaining Your Credential

Upon successful completion of your exam, you will be granted your Project Management Professional (PMP)® designation. In order for your PMP to remain active, you will need achieve 60 professional development units (PDUs) every three years. PDUs are reported through PMI's Continuing Certification Requirements System (CCRS) located on PMI.org.

PMI has launched The PMI Talent Triangle® as a way to categories your PDUs:

- Technical project management
- Leadership
- Strategic and business management

For the PMP, you need to earn:

- Education: a minimum of eight PDUs in each of the three categories, with a total minimum of 35 PDUs out of the 60 coming from education
- Giving Back (volunteering, creating knowledge, and working as a professional): a maximum of 25 PDUs with no more than eight coming from working as a professional.

Questions or Comments?

I'd love to hear your thoughts, feedback, and/or recommendations on this PMP® Pocket Guide. Contact me at BelindaGoodrich.com.

Interested in having me speak at your next event?

I deliver high-impact keynotes and workshops on all aspects of project management: project risk management, practical project management, engaging stakeholders, conflict resolution, and emotional intelligence for project managers. Contact me at BelindaGoodrich.com.

Need additional study resources?

Be sure to check out PMLearningSolutions.com for all of your PMP® exam preparation needs.

Belinda Goodrich
PMP, PMI-RMP, PMI-SP, PgMP, PMI-ACP, CAPM

PM Speaker   PM Expert   PM Author

BelindaGoodrich.com

Globally recognized as a project management expert, Belinda Goodrich is the founder and CEO of The Goodrich Institute and PM Learning Solutions. PM Learning Solutions, formerly known as Passionate Project Management, is focused on delivering world-class project management exam preparation programs and materials. Under The Goodrich Institute, Belinda serves as a consultant to a number of Fortune 500 companies with a focus on improving the project management processes and practices in order to drive business growth.

After over 20 years of corporate project management and executive leadership experience, Belinda "retired" to serve the project management community. The first woman in the world to achieve five of the PMI credentials, Belinda now holds the following: PMP®, CAPM®, PMI-SP®, PMI-ACP®, PMI-RMP®, PgMP®. In addition, Belinda is a Certified Scrum Master.

The author of multiple books and courseware on project management and PMI exam topics, Belinda is an in-demand facilitator, speaker, and consultant. As an instructor, Belinda has helped thousands of project managers achieve their project management credentials. Her passion is creating the connection between theoretical project management concepts and real-world business needs through energetic and engaging sessions.

In 2018, Belinda will be releasing a co-authored book *The Will to Win* with famed leadership experts Jim Cathcart and Brian Tracy. In addition, her soon-to-be released book *SHIFT: Business Growth through Exceptional Project Management* is already garnering positive attention from industry leaders.

PMLearningSolutions.com

BelindaGoodrich.com

Download the PMP Application Assistant Spreadsheet for FREE at:

PMLearningSolutions.com/pmp-spreadsheet

 "Love this tool!!! This made the application process so much easier! Thank you!!"

View the PMP Concepts Learning Series for FREE at:

PMLearningSolutions.com/pmp-concepts-learning-series

 "Thank you…this series has been a tremendous help in studying for my PMP!"

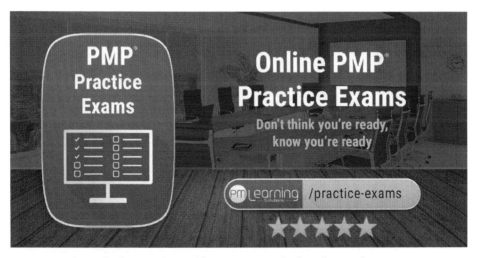

Additional Resources

PMP®/CAPM® Exam Prep Training Courses

10% OFF using promo code AMAZON10

View course schedule at pmLearning Solutions

Special offer for purchasers of this Pocket Guide!

10% Off of any PMP/CAPM Exam Prep Training Course.

Use promo code AMAZON10 at checkout on PMLearningSolutions.com

 "PMLS provided our company with excellent preparation for the PMP Exam during an onsite class. This was probably the best PM class I've taken. The instructor kept the entire room tuned with interest for the entire course."

 "I recently attended Belinda's PMP Training, And All I can say is "WOW" She has created a unique training system, that clearly sets the pace against any other training I've attended! Among some of those others are top area colleges. If you're looking to get the PMP under your belt ... Attending Belinda's course is a must!"

 "I highly recommend PM Learning Solutions for your qualification and certification preparation without reservation. Belinda goes above and beyond to ensure that the class, as well as the individual, understands the materials and is prepared to take the exam. She points out the nuances of the exam and reinforces those learnings with real examples. Could not have asked for a better experience. Two thumbs way up for PM Learning Solutions!"

51909315R00039

Made in the USA
Columbia, SC
23 February 2019